Thought Balloon

Thought Balloon

Kit Robinson

ROOF BOOKS
NEW YORK

ISBN: 978-1-931824-79-8

Library of Congress Control Number: 2019930950

Author photograph by Eric Breitbard.

Some of these poems have appeared in the following publications: *Annex Press, The Canary Islands Connection, Cordite Review, Dispatches from the Poetry Wars, Elderly, The End of the World, Have Your Chill, Lana Turner, Nowhere, Poem in Your Pocket* (Berkeley Public Library), *PoetryNow* (Poetry Foundation), *Project for Innovative Poetry, Resist Much/Obey Little,* and *WayBay* (BAMPFA). Thanks to the editors.

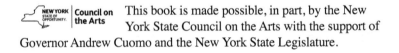

This book is made possible, in part, by the New York State Council on the Arts with the support of Governor Andrew Cuomo and the New York State Legislature.

Roof Books
are published by
Segue Foundation
300 Bowery, New York, NY 10012
seguefoundation.com

Roof Books
are distributed by
Small Press Distribution
1341 Seventh Street
Berkeley, CA. 94710-1403
800-869-7553 or spdbooks.org

CONTENTS

On the Sound

CROW VALLEY

Goes away a long time
Comes back to think of it
The sky is how deep
Sun through Doug fir
Open up the throttle a little

This kind of rhyming goes back to the cave
Today only teenage girls can crawl through
Big rigs on the roads carrying nearly everything
Guy drags boxes on dolly down ramp
Early morning delivery

Smooth passage through the inner ear
Time with the lights on
Indolent instants on the boat of Ra
Hopping across islands in the sound
Hear the mighty engine's roar

Beginnings are numberless
An end leaves one gasping for air
You don't have to do this
But you can't do anything else
The occasional car stops and turns

Families arrive from parts elsewhere
Science nudges the unknown
Two things from which men must avert their gaze
Death and the face of the sun
Day's first erasure ripples the morning surface

They are looking for a cup of coffee
The flag flutters in a light breeze
All this is true but still
Meaning ekes out a living
The birds are more than happy to oblige

The voice has scales the locals know by ear
When you get to the harbor you are there
In the heat of the day
Time is something unexpected
Like a motorcyclist removing her helmet

WEST SOUND

Sticking up out of the water
Covered in fir, hemlock, cedar and pine
These islands
Wake with the sun
Where the continent breaks
Against the Northern Pacific
Without a word

Wind in the branches
The feel of it on the face
Elegiac intervals
Between sounds
Light on porch rails
Casting shadows
Even in advance

A landscape of calls
Very little to go on
As if waiting for a train of thought
Inner and outer realms
Coincide
If only for a moment
First boat out into the water

MOUNT CONSTITUTION

Bright red geraniums
A wake up call
For Mr. Loose and Unnecessary

Gather strength in batches
The idea goes one way
Awake, a walk in a field

Sessions in space
Kick off the covers
Neighborly glances

Situate yourself
For the ride across the sky
Sometimes it's chilly

Boats tied up
To the dock
Like so many parenthetical asides

She and her dog
Down the road
Before breakfast

Leaves on the vine
The breeze makes quiver
Are models of flexibility

Let nothing happen for a while
And surely it will
Despite your best efforts

The thinking is
Clouds gather to west
A combination of elements

Near miss offshoot
Arrange the letters
A fortune in shipbuilding

The matter at hand
Neither here nor there
Compared to making a living

Imagine a concert
Convened every morning
Shorebirds of the Pacific rim

Plenty of energy
The turn to luggage
Time to pull up stakes

And there you have it
To have and to have not
Some like it hot

People moving about
You big lug
A sign of perpetual vacancy

Just let yourself in
Chill waters of delight
Family members on the pier

A light feeling of expectation
Stick to the plan
A breath of fresh air

FALSE BAY

Words in place of fingers
Sky in place of heart
Sound in place of memory
Whales in place of harmonicas
Liberals in place of precipices
Door in place of tree
Sensuality in place of remuneration
Number in place of color
Eyes in place of sea hawks
September in place of time

Inside the cave
Outside the bar
Whenever it suits you
Unless there is a fire
Until the last minute
Without being aware
Because of the noise
Under the circumstances
On top of the fridge
By the side of the road

Ceremonial embouchure
Leaseway tires
Probabilistic septuagenarians
Semi-automatic doubt
Consensual sacrifice
Inter-island plasticity
Roadside realism
Drowsy blandishments
Tonal arrival
Misbegotten hallelujah

Art is the last refuge of polygamists
Rail transport is the badminton of hungry ghosts
Sensitivity is the germ warfare of electric guitars
Language is the roulette of pacifism
Cinema is the cliff face of adolescence
Melancholy is the nasturtium of time
Outer space is the typewriter of misapprehension
Ostentation is the oatmeal of fellowship
Everyday life is the climate change of introspection
Horticulture is the guardian angel of sex

DECEPTION PASS

As darkness falls in the mountains
A dim glimmer of history slips the mind
Fog in the crotch between rises
Other side of the lake

Once a self-made man
Who started from scratch
Became governor
Then a shipbuilding empire
When the doctors warned he'd die of stress
He bought a large parcel on Orcas Island
Moved there with his family
Lived another 25 years
Ceding the land to the state
For use by the public
Building roads and bridges himself
When state funds proved inadequate
Until finally the National Park Service came through
Today you can stand at the top
A limestone tower at the summit
With a view of Mount Baker across the sound

Another a pioneering loner
Farmed on Whidbey Island
Commuted by boat to Port Townsend
Where he was postmaster general
Was killed and beheaded by Indians
In proxy retaliation
For the murder by whites of a tribal chief

Now the lake is almost entirely white
Fog reflected in its rain dimpled surface
Dark white
Or what you might call silver
Before the deep green shadows of the mountainsides

STORM KING

It's the 40s again
Welcome back
Jitterbug clarinet mornings
Snappy vocalese
Up 'n' at 'em attitude
A slap on the backside of fate
Off we go
Into the wild blue yonder
Until the dining room fills
With decades before and since

Good night Mrs. Calabash wherever you are
The snap from the fireplace
Here is where you lodge your complaints
One line at a time
The way a drawing takes shape
The shapes of mountains
Clouds and a lake
Wind moving light on the surface
Of a life
Which brings us to where we sit

Nestled between peaks
Ferns all about and tall firs covered in moss
Such are the pleasures of description
A kind of neutrality like Switzerland
That allows us to be with the immediate environment
And also not
Because busy making notes
On mirrors for others to read later
Okay kids let's go
Leaving so soon?

That's great news because time is ticking away
Footsteps behind me
A day of not drinking
Trails up into the interior
Laughter from up the way
And that casual, rascally counter tempo
That sings its way through our capillaries
For generations
Even after the departure
Of the vintage auto rally

BELLTOWN

Silent forms
Break into fugitive night
The caper drama
Squeezing between raindrops
A city is as its citizens make it
At street level
Or up in the air

Traffic patterns
A natural bridge
Icons of the light rail system
Connecting ramen
To Latin jazz
Where feet do the walking
And talk is entirely free

One step beyond anticipation
What happens matters
It shakes the whole body
Out of habit
And into intensity
One passionate doorway
Some special ground floor

Earth Sense

RASPBERRIES IN JANUARY

When lizards grow feathers
Sky clouds over
Temperatures drop
World goes hurtling through space
Put affairs in order
Dress casually
Order chow mein to bring home

The light at the end of the tunnel
Is light green
There are no wrong notes
Only a few conventioneers and tourists drinking quietly
The kids call scare quotes "scrunchy peace"
We join the animals
It is a pleasure to say the least

MONKISH

Corrugated lifespan
Tailored cords
A drink in one hand
Untangle the cable
Purified air

Turn on before opening envelopes
Same size as last week
Jangle of piano innards
Stretched across a bay
The rippling of fans

First, walk
Later, dance on air
There are sentences sound doesn't mess with
So silent they are written into the body
Then, head for the door

THOUGHT BALLOON

Translation isn't the half of it
The same impulse animates dirt
To silently capture these moments
While so much else goes by unnoticed
Look out the window at your mind
That's what I'm talking about
Life in the present imperfect

Sit facing Japan
Vague light on bamboo
The Hohenzollerns never had it so good
I just thought you'd like to know
King of Prussia Mall is nearly three million square feet
The flaw in the Navaho rug is intentional
Hats off to the Great Spirit

Need to sweep up in here
Open the gates to the city
Coal dust covers everything
Condense into one solid brick
To represent our common crisis
Hands across the stratosphere
Hyper-conductivity rules

Emptiness is the mother of all
A patch of dirt a few seeds
Vast civilizations prosper
The timekeeper's tears keep flowing
Everything that can go wrong does
Yet we persist
Leaves the size of elephants' ears only green

OPEN, TO LOVE

For Paul Bley

Tenderness written by hand
Think of all the ways we can fail!
Stop practicing
Simply perform and record
This is the big time
The time of your life
Watching rain drops
Suspended in air
Land on the walkway
To tomorrow

And so turn another corner
With sadness as its boutonniere
And sweetness as its grapefruit
Because we are gone in that moment
And only too eager for another taste
If we have taste it is only for stones
Light on puddles
Swoosh of tires
An amalgam of affect brimming like a sea
As if we were making all this up

Stay inside the boat
One of many wise sayings that come to mind
The river is wide
Neither have I
The wings to fly
On down the line
The line is a unit of joy
Like a popsicle
But that is preposterous
Because it takes too long to say

It is strange to be gone in a moment
Between Canada and Florida
Falls the shadow
A kind of linger
About a hand's breadth apart
And climbing
The light fades
The garrulous forms persist
Meeting out justice in all the old familiar spaces
Ones our heads could never get used to

Open, to love
A space we can inhabit
Structures that fall into place
Momentarily speaking
Which is nothing if not surprising
Like cutting up vegetables for soup
The knock of the knife
Wood that comes like a tree
From having been there
And knowing where we go from here

TRANSBLUENCY

The poem doesn't care who writes it
It is waiting in the wings
A belt of ekphrastic energy circumnavigating the earth
The planet we are made of
While others struggle to be fastened down completely
By standard protocols of identity and access management
We enter an archway and just keep walking
It's good exercise
As opposed to war, pollution, greed, hate and delusion
Though these certainly have their adherents

I is a sum total adding up to now
Subject to future operations
Add to, subtract from, multiply by, divide by
And drive by
Trailing a long history like a tail
Reaching back into the paleo
There's no place like magma
When it comes time to relax
And think it over
But we are too busy being multiples

The fountain draws from many streams
By way of the existence of cities
Shoots its spray to the heavens
In Technicolor and black and white
This experience of seeing
Is basic to being both awake and asleep
An insertion just beneath the skin
A workshop just beneath the floor
Water beneath the surface of the earth
Darkness

Transformation is natural
Woman to man, man to woman
The long road to being
The butterfly's return
Silence where before there was none
The poem does not let go
It arrives from the future incessantly
Ordinary fingers pick up on its cascade of plans
We can see it from here
A head with stars for eyes

To play extremely slowly
Is to caress the surface of time
To speed to abolish its domain
Cheer up my brothers and sisters
And walk in the sunshine
Our understanding is so very great
Being beyond the comprehension of a single mind
Life forms outstrip the rigorous calisthenics of calculation
Populate the ocean floor

THE TEMPORARY SITUATION

I got a friend request on brain book
Inured, is that a word?
Comments by Thursday
Talk to the hand
It's been a hard day's journey into night

Even in the beginning there is a feeling
Walking and talking for miles on end
To be idiomatic in a vacuum
It is a shining thing
Baron von Tollbooth and the Chrome Nun

It's getting so I can't even hear myself think
Drifting along with the tumbling tumbleweeds
And pack a lantern in case of blackout
Because the beach is right down the street
And anything can happen

You learn something every day
The way certain people have of moving
The shift from major to minor
The collective buzz
The temporary situation

As if any instance could be any other way
Thousands of answers to questions never asked
The long rain of centuries
Bathing the streets in light
So long until we meet again

INDEPENDENT SUSPENSION

Birds in their honorary vests
Make public for the first time
Their constitutional calls
Papers gather dust
Houses strain after paint jobs
Lawns grow, only to be mown
The sight of a boat on the water
Making fast for land
Cheers us up
Like a letter from Beauty to the Beast

Lines in the heat of battle
Get crossed
Down the mountain and onto a table of air
Separate situations evolve differently
News travels light
No kung fu or soccer for two weeks
Okay to swim
Command lines for pause and resume
A sequence of alternations
That lasts a lifetime

Burnt edges of things in the mind's eye
A riot of color
From moment to moment
You go away and come back
A conversational embrace
A five-mile hike
A jar of change
An old address book
The last time I saw you
The warmth of the sun

A fracture is a learning moment
The world comes apart at the seems
As has always been the case
So we sit up straight on earth
Get down before all division
If only for a little while
A walk around the block
An electric train
A vision of loveliness
The time it takes to come back and go

You have to be very patient
Because there is nothing
Flash of the spirit
In a dark forest
Voices from next door
Tabula rasa
Smooth as silk
When in the course of human events
There is a native sound
That impels us to open the door

SEPARATIONS IN SPACE

Holistic prescriptions
From Mother Africa
Stir the mind
The spirit like a spark in the forest
Tap tap on the high hat
Listen for signals
On the trunk of a tree
Skin dry
The hands worked to a fine tenor
Doctor Wichita at your service

Continents in disarray
The repercussions of colonialism
Continue to play themselves out
In tragedy and in farce
Looming near the surface
So anyone can understand
Who walks the walk of humans
No water, no bread, no peace
Now to be gone once and fly
Where speech unhooks and goes wide

Not ready for democracy they call it
And bring back the generals
The tree out the window is a particular olive
Bearing no fruit
Still in the removal of light
Evidence is always of something
Evenly spaced across a cloud bank
Theory has it the east is red
But the state is a creature of policy
Whereas people mill about

More and more there is the impulse to connect
Separations in space
A landscape more dope than rope
I bet you don't even know what I'm saying
Said one man
We get together every now and then and jam
The dream of the ancient mariner
Open the portholes
Leaves now backlit dark before darkening sky
Alive in the very quick

MARKS ON PAPER

Marks on paper
Are all that matter
To a person lost
To the world
If only for a moment
When comes a knock
On the door
And in comes someone
Who needs help
Dressing a wound

So much trouble
In the world
Is ours to redress
But the poem is not
The place to address
All that is injured
Sick and tired
Except by way
Of letters
Their recombinant DNA

Incontrovertible
Improvisatory
Imagistic
Interior
Illuminated
In light of all that
Goes on around us
A jacket of letters
To walk around in
Wind picks up

I don't know what to say
Everything will be happy and sad
Rage builds up
Topples civilizations
Eons later
Bricks in the road
A new generation
Reorganizes your phone
Gene sequencing
Makes very little noise

What can be assigned a number
That which cannot
Something swims out
The drift of cigarette smoke
From off camera
In an interview
From the 60s
A contemplative moment
No one is laughing
Then they do

GARCIA ROAD SCREED

America has intermarried
Wake up
Do not fall prey
The concept of the blank page
Is history
Each moment is embedded
In story
What is yours
They interweave with the best of us
Doors open

Then song enters the picture
An ear in the mind of a worm
Torn up about outer space
I Know About The Life
A low ratio of signal to noise
In the sound of Archie Shepp
The song is "Well You Needn't"
Held over for performance
In different heads
Falling through time

You can make your own pages
Coffee is the work of many backs
Hauling beans across continents
The air is thick
Dust of copulas covers the earth
We drive right down to the Ocean
Glide along the beach
Body surf on syllabic waves
Air circulates above the surface of the planet
Succulents persist

SEEING AS HOW

Seeing as how
You don't know what you don't know
Rhymes arrive by special delivery
With mobile, global and white-label options
Because the day is long
As long as you're up
And tells a story
As long as your arm
The sense of duration
Is illusory
When you come to think of it
Because nothing lasts forever
And we are gathered here together
On the head of a pin
So start walking

Neither a broadcaster nor a listener be
But walk directly home
Head down, hands in pockets
Take in the dog and put out the cat
Probably do this early a.m. here
So maybe midnight there
As the world turns over
And goes back to sleep
Under cloud cover
Like a false clue in a detective book

Wind against the sun in windows
Opens a trap door to memory
By being there first
A neat trick
The width and breadth of a continent

Where am I in all this?
A poem could last a whole day
Its stresses can stress you out
If you're not careful
You can't be too careful
Are you putting me on?
Put another record on
Put a jacket
I'm sitting on a low wall on 10th Street writing this
    on my phone
That's where

What about the reader?
Where is she?
What's on the line is immediacy
Divided by contingency
Equals transitivity
A key property of both partial order relations
And equivalence relations
According to *Wikipedia*
Let's stop here and rest a minute
The world is large
And cannot be taken in at a glance
But we are on top of it
Sitting side by side
On a front porch swing
On the Continental Divide

From here the ocean looks endless
Bottom line: many fishes
For fishes no end to water
For birds no end to air
For humans no end to talking
Walking and talking

Taking things as they come
Other points of interest
Other lines of thought
Other planes of there

SOME TIME AFTER

After suffering a great loss
A strong feeling of harmony
Lifts the body into space
The space-time continuum
That is our home

RESISTANCE IS JOY

Resistance is joy
A watched pot does too boil eventually
Keep up the pressure
For this we wake and
Drop the hammer

Abandon all hope oh ye who enter these
  hallowed out hells
Delusions are inexhaustible
The demons are running the show
There is nothing so simple as a simple sentence
Lasting 140 bad characters and no time at all

And leaves a bitter taste in the head
We don't want no fascist groove thang
Always call them on their lies
When thieves rule the world
Only the outcast is trustworthy

GREETINGS FROM THE EDGE

For Norman and Kathie

Deep inside the marine layer
Nothing but rain, wind and fog
Not to mention grammar
The grammar of dreams
Between the covers of a book
Read long ago
In a foreign city

How long how long
The delicate vastness of indecipherability
The earth accedes to the watery onslaught
The runoff enters the ocean
Greetings from the edge
As far away as possible without exiting entirely
Clinging to the continent

The sleep of reason produces monsters
Liars, thieves, tyrants, bullies, charlatans
Who prize only money and power
Care not at all for human beings
To say nothing of the earth
Her flora, fauna, water and air
Now poised at a delicate balance

Oceanic systems move slowly
A hummingbird still in rainy midair
The life of the turtle one hundred years
Time is neither here nor there
The cat cries out for attention
Life and death do not rhyme
The sky is white

Elephants, geishas, turtles, Buddhas, whales
Beets, flowers, eggs, starfish, lions
The mind is restless
Always looking for something
A list of things to do under heavy rain
Time is under development
Space is upside down

EARTH SENSE

For Rachel Carson and Agnes Martin

Inspiration grows out of the earth
A garden of earthly delights
Always just around the corner
On your way to the store
Change jingles in your pocket
Life rides along in your bag
What's most worthy of analysis
Is what falls out of them
Your inadvertent asides
Tentative tenuous subtle supple under the breath

This command and control environment
Is made for TV
Not for you and me
We are otherwise
Non-compliant with the panicky strictures
   of inflated dominance
To the toxic fantasies of prize assholes trailing
   fake-news ties
We prefer the continuous, borderless, microtonal,
   transnational flow
Otherwise known as reality
As in keep it real, Homes
Remember, this earth is our joint hood

Let's save all beings, ok?
This land is made for sensitive beings of every color
   and stripe
Not just a small club of fascist thugs and their
   billionaire keepers
I mean really, come on!
But where was I?

The sun still shines on the local garden
It bounces off the pavement and puts a spring in your step
There are people to see, sounds to identify, thoughts
   to entertain
There is dinner to shop for and cook, kids and grownups
   to check in on
Let me know when you have a minute

Imperfection is everywhere
All your efforts fall short
Disappointment, frustration reign
Our idea of it is unattainable
Yet altogether it is perfectly all right
When seen in a certain light
The light of a distant campfire
Sulphur light, diagonal light
Opal light & old light & marsh light & moonlight
Thanks, inspirational friendship, for lighting the way

The sea around us is an inspiration any child
   can understand
A physical delight
Energy stored in battery harmony, open for all to hear
Alternate pages turn quickly when no one is looking
If you are shocked you must have been asleep
Something can be reality or TV, never both
Mistakes are the saints' way of messing with us
If only we could see the future, but we have our backs to it
Turn around, look out and live
That is the message in the bottle

Way off on the horizon a distant plume of smoke
The eye sees what the mind cannot grasp
Turning over in space
We are alive to the half of it
Let's order in and go through the game plan once again

It's going to be a long, hard slog
We better get started
There isn't much time
The mind is a collective breathing
Our direction has never been more clear

HULI HULI CHICKEN

Local color, vermilion
A cardinal's crest
Ginger hanging near continuous ground
The wind picks up where you left off
You locked yourself out
And now are at the mercy of the fates
Fortunately there are many of them
Destiny is a quail
Alighting on a branch
Part of the flowering continuity
Born of the passage of time

Tom is in Italy
The incremental benefits are large
Business talk poolside
While millions dodge immigration police
Having colonized the rest of world
Wreaking havoc on native populations everywhere
The western powers now withdraw behind a defunct
    nationalism
They serve up a dangerous cocktail of fear and rage
We all feel it
And admire the visual indifference of birds and fish

Everywhere we go we let off heat
To the north where the rainclouds gather
To the south where the sun is god
To the east where rivers run down to the sea
To the west where canyons shine purple and gold
Our names have been mixed with those of plants
    and herbs
Our hands are steady on the wheel
Our hearts are in the right place

Our brains are more supple than any computer
This is why we have called you to witness

Somewhere along the way
A slight change in the angle of descent
A break in the clouds
A wide view of the prevailing landscape
A red bird on a high branch
The big rheostat in the sky
Turns all the way up for a moment then slightly down
A length of thought
Stretched between the fence posts of day
As well known as butterfly or spider

THE THIN MAN GOES HOME

You are as even tempered as a frying pan
In a sudden downpour
A campsite in disarray
A long time coming
Laughter from two yards over
The neighborhood a claim on space
Involving multiple parties

It must be Father's Day
Judging by the heightened attentions of daughters
    and sons
Thus a man enjoys solitude, stillness, pink petals of
    the carrier rose
And in a certain light
The sonic continuum of tires against the road
The sensation of being carried along toward the end of
    a sentence
After the disappearance of the period

Air to breathe, water to drink
The suggestion box is empty
Obsolete equipment piles up in nooks and crannies
This is all wrong, that's messed up
We go on in and make ourselves comfortable
The movie has just begun
It's Nick and Nora Charles and their little dog Asta

They're visiting Nick's parents in the suburbs
He's on the wagon and trying to keep a low profile
But of course she brags about him to the local paper
And soon he's embroiled in detective work despite himself
There is crime everywhere, even here in the suburbs
It must be human nature
Desperate characters on the loose

"Yoke yourself to your strongest conviction"
Was a piece of advice derived from the Y in JOY
But Pam doesn't buy that
And I say it sounds too slavish
Remember the Groucho line
"These are my principles
If you don't like them, I have others"

When the pen runs out of ink
You simply replace the cartridge
And continue writing
To the sound of jet planes overhead
It's time to revive the typewriter
For the benefit of kids
Now entering the ranks of the scribe force

Sliding the paper under the roller
Striking the surface with heavy metal blows
History curls right into the future
A Möbius strip
That brings bygone media around and back
With all the drama, character, sound, light and destiny
Alive in an imagination of living

LINSEED OIL

i.m John Ashbery

Seriously though, I don't think you comprehend
The magnitude of what we're looking at
Not enough pairs of white socks
The sounds of crows cawing behind us
Plans without maps
Maps without sufficient colors
As if our employment were merely temporary
Which I suppose it is
Like everything else in this joint

Hard to emerge from the long shadow of the master
Possibly impossible
A breeze picks up
Feeble sunlight grazes the leaves
The air smacks of distant fires
But we can still breathe
Then change into something more comfortable
You better believe it
Poking at memory with a stick

Who goes there?
Lend me your ears
Rome was not built overnight
Nothing better to do
In which case forget it
Time is an elastic band
For wrapping cables when you tear down the set
Easy to speak lightly of it later
Hard to save while using

What we say to each other
Should be plain and wide

Like a body at rest
But gets tripped up
In the welter of everything else
Not a bad thing
When you consider the great escape
Into thin air
Of our impressions

The wherewithal gets lost en route
The color of alphabet soup
Soon everyone is picking favorites
Or pushing up daisies
As the case may be
A case each of red and white vocabularies
To be opened whenever the spirit moves one
Early and often
Or after they've all gone home

An Ordinary Umbrian Morning

For James & Deborah & Ahni

PHRASES FROM A MANUAL OF STYLE

Assign to each number a color
One black
Two white
Three red
Four yellow
Five blue
Six green
Seven orange
Eight purple
Nine brown

Ten silver
Do same thing with animals
The phrases that float into place from who knows where
The night is long and will have to be covered
By a body at rest
One leg draped over the side
For the longest time
I thought you were there beside me
Then realized you'd fled to the other room
Leaving me to grapple with my insomnia

A sequence of hill towns each with its special wines,
    meats, leather goods
Art and architecture
The palace afloat on a cloud high above the village
    at sunset
Came back a different way
Tourism is rapid eye movement
By other means
Napoleon takes the same walk every time
Dereliction of duty
Sensitive curious and chaste
Phrase happy

Several centuries later we teeter on the brink
It feels like it
The polar icecaps are melting
Into our coke zero
Fires consume the western states
Hurricanes batter the south
Quakes shake Mexico
Plastic manacles ensnare Pacific whales
What more proof do you want
Of climatastrophe

On an ordinary Umbrian morning
Quiet overtakes the crew
In after coffee exercise routines
The pen is a kind of flute
The flute a drum for keeping time
The book a mystery
The body spread wide in Tai Chi
The double c is a hard c
As in Pinocchio
The Sanfatucchio Giant roams the lakeside

Colors rifle through memory
Nights clothed in silence
Phrases from a manual of style
History resting on a hilltop
Coming into view
Coming to think of it
Returning to the scene of the crime
History is a crying shame
Racking up points on a map
Coming to light in the planes of a familiar face

IN MEDIAS RES

Hand me my subjectivity will you?
God only knows what I'd be without you
Brian Wilson, a proper name
Categories dislodge in a hail of empirical bullets
We add things up as we go along
Color is a bonding agent
Sun on the hilltops
Lines of blank cuts in the stones
A world of angles in the town square
Hard to remember which photo is which

The letter c pronounced hard, soft or chewy
Language is a form of agreement
Let me in, wee-oop
An imaginary Napoleon batters down the doors to Europe
Mysteries of the Arctic Circle
The world and its streets, people
What a consideration
A word for nothing
As Eigner has indicated
Tumbling along with the tumbling tumbleweeds

In medias res, our permanent address
A storyline is a jail of bedposts
The Battle of New Orleans, Lonnie Donnegan version
Down the Mississippi to the Gulf of Mexico
Sun bouncing between hills out the car window
A movable feat
To string beads in retrospect
While open for business
The business of America
History is a bunk bed

Forgot to look at the clock
Margaret Cavendish, Catherine of Siena, Teresa of Avila
Intelligent matter, an invisible ring, a close sharing
   between friends
Enjoy the rest of your visit
Determined to walk upright
Walking and talking
Before and after sleep
A slip of the tongue
A clear view
A reason to believe

ONTOLOGICAL ACOUSTICS

Being is too lazy to rehearse
Receptive if standing apart
The tang of fall weather
In a glass of water
Phenomena, clearly backlit
The world is smooth
Only when seen from space
A faint noise then the grand approach
While you were out
Another life springs to our attention

Will you be here till I get back?
A slight breeze, a guttered candle, a short walk
Up and down stone stairs
With coffee in one hand
A reminder of Peru
Bolivar's preemptive strike
Maneuvers high in the Andes
The dog wants in
The poem is a kind of bark
Stripped from a tree, on which to depart

Suddenly time stands still
Only to move off into the crowd
Reabsorbing the sounds of metallic tools
That measure our given forms of labor
We stands for development
A continuous stream of interaction
Down through the ages
Out onto the street
Voices ring out against stone
The soft passages of the inner ear

The Rolling Stones, a well-oiled machine
Sympathy for the lived
Experience, a bump in the road
Question marks line up for the main meal
What color is that you are wearing?
When swifts dive from a tower
Let's meet at the square
Find out what everyone is talking about
I could get used to this
If not otherwise engaged

The football we have today isn't violent enough
You dropped a bomb on me
Hope springs external
A stitch in the side of time
The Mediterranean Basin reverberates
In melodic minor
Can we go now?
Finish your lesson
I prefer not to
Hung up on the flipside of sleep

HIGH BASTION

Some to be soon
Some later for that
A tankard for scale
The key on the hook
Absolutely irrelevant
The blind old dog underfoot
But still let in after all
A fellow creature on limited time
Here a couple of budding musicians
There a pair of wandering scholars

These hill towns built on tumulus grounds
Draw water from deep wells
Keep talk to a maximum
Of phrase wars met for millennia
Keep your eye on the sparrow
Your hand on the plow
Later we'll taste the new vintage
On a bench in the old square
Duck when believing any rumor
The people were smaller then

Light and shade fall diagonal on the pages of a book
The one you are writing with eyes closed
The saints line up to adore the virgin
Her squeaky clean bambino
Fall breezes snap you to attention
The dust above the road
Porcini, truffles, tomatoes, onion, garlic, pasta
Tagliatelle vision
Elevates the pulse
Juicing the race, human

An iron bar affixed to the wall at a diagonal
Above horses for structural support
Their rumps reimagined by Piero
Lances approximately parallel
Or crossed at random angles
Trill of victory, angina of defeat
Nobility bottled and put up
In cool cellar
By Benedictine monks
Saint Francis comes before the Sultan

Now that everything has been said and done
Let's share a jug of fresh water
And resupply our fading memory cells
Through the study of onomastics
When what's-his-name met what's-her-name
On the plains of hesitation
Just before a good nap
Soon we will be able to stand up straight
And take a few steps
And go to the corner for coffee

The people united will never be defeated
Unless we sell ourselves into slavery
To the lowest bidder
Get up, stand up
Wake up and live
Carry your country across itself
Spastic if you like, but close
Enter an originary office
Chest first
To make of the moment a fleet of starry ships

Maker's Mark

ROOM TEMP

Time goes by
Fires on river taxi
Years later
There on video
Rest of world suffering
Easy chair reupholster
Backhanded compliment
Pearl handled revolvers
Dawn on
Back in a jiffy

Go on without
Kluge together a brain
Lunch spots break out
Air tastes of *as*
The something else
We only just realized
What with property
Always a few hands
Connections fizzle
Bass drum time

See you there
Like your hair
Light on bamboo
Time of your life
An opening in the forest
Forest floor
Conversation with snake
All surface
Back in time for
Lend a hand to

Adjustable seating
What friends are
Early innings
Only in theory
Keep playing
Turn at light
Moving targets
Lines intersect
Too big too small
Missing the point

Temporary closure
On wings of dove
No soap radio
Cracker barrel logic
Staticky signal
Hum in head
Eyes light on object
Of fascination
Returns the favor
Moves over

HOLOGRAM

Write on wall
In blood
Under water
On the edge
Of all thinking
Because of what?
The bright flavor of air
Crowning the cube
Easy as pie
Skin of all living

THE WORLD AS WHAT HAVE YOU

For Will Alexander

World matter rolling
Dense spectacles
Gigantic metropoli
Wherein the mind
The luminous hydrocarbon
Of flesh and blood
A roar without a lion
The abstract truth
Read and remembered again

Without percussion
The voice sails
Lost in the head
An embouchure of rails
Windward harmonics
A gigantic intensity
Startled into life
Blunt statement of fact
In an elevated state

Visions trace rudiments
Letters escaping words
On backs of authors
Sighs of relief
An imagination of seeming
All space
Vast galactic prospects
Operatic integers
A brazen aspect

ROOM TONE

The meanings of things
Get lost
In an inside out capacity

Similar to situations
Viewed on TV

You think you can
Then walk away
Pretending to be someone else

Take off
Into thin air

Leave behind
What you know
In favor of what you don't

Where ends meet
Beginning to make sense

A world out there
Asymptotic curves
Totemic figures

Fetishistic images
Common ground

Remember to buy coffee
Find books for friend
Get back to work

All impulse tends to matter
Meaning where you put it

The big picture
Needs must have a frame
Even Steven

Attention strays
Love on the assembly line

An ode to bodies in space
Cream jeans
Crop photo

A lookalike
Standing in for

A forest of timpani
Sounding the bay
In the head for miles

Pull up to the curb
Let passengers out

You have all day
The winds of change
Whip up a shake

Percussion drives the van
There is your continuity

A present to be opened later
In case of fire
Break glass

The signs of the times
In all caps

LAST THINGS FIRST

Last blast of cold air
Last song on airwaves
Last clink in bowl
Last voices from beyond the pale
Last symbolism
Last black jacket, black shirt, silver tie
Last black velvet suit
Last flute flutter high above the fray
Last waiting to go
Last edge of moon through scattered clouds

Things have got to change
Things have a hold on you
Things like this are never easy
Things will be better bye and bye
Things will be all right
Things will continue
Things are never simple
Things called by the wrong names
Things leaning against a wall
Things my mother taught me

First in first out
First to speak is Coyote
First I hear one voice then many
First lady of the opera Maria Callas
First look at the new crop
First get it right
First base, who's on?
First time ever I saw your face
First in the hearts of his countrymen
First dress then get in the car and go

THE MORNING LINE

You get up
To take up
The line

Only just
Aware enough
To hear

Voices in air
Devoid of whereabouts
Interested only in sound

What is
Overflows
The thought of it

Has many sides
Ten thousand
To be exact

Moments of identification
Begin with a body
At home or work

Possessions adhere
In a restricted economy
Under the sign

Capital I
But when you come
Face to face

With another
An absolutely other
All bets are off

And you incline
To the diagonal
Whereon the unknown

Tips the scales
In favor of
A reappraisal

Of all that has come before
A whiff of ozone
Signaling rain

An interruption
In your constitution
One morning

A text
From beyond the pale
Not the whole story

But a line of verse
That recurs
At interesting intervals

Like a month of Sundays
Until everything that is
Turns over

Goes back to sleep
In no time at all
Because it's more than that

BE BOP

In walking
You pass the post
A marker
Along the stage line
Site of anticipation
And retrospect
Two sides of no coin

The present a flip
In mid-air
Tingles of light
And sound thinking
Here we are
Making it happen
While also concerned

Over this 'n' that
Hovers over the other
The thing we'd forgot
In our haste to arrive
On the beat
A flavor
Of sudden knowledge

You say one thing
I think elsewise
What's real?
The gap
A promise to connect
In the flesh
Outside on the street

Getting going
Having it out
Having them over
Looking at the plans
Rolling a joint
Looking at the weather
Going to Oakland

MISTERIOSO

Time is scenes
Cut the deck
And lay the cards down one by one
You represent a strand of life
Trailing back into the Pleistocene
No one knows the future
Everything always ends up otherwise

The air is alive
With predatory creatures
That give you the heebie-jeebies
A flash of light
In the dark ages
A team of research scientists
Can't explain

BODY ENGLISH

Poetry taught me how to listen
You can't say everything at once

Who here is exhausted
Too tired to raise their head

Music teaches us to see
Out the back of a truck

The artist is at home in her studio
Sentences learned in school

The street flattens them
Traffic is a big equalizer

The arch at the small of the back
The shoulders rolling with the night

Silence of memory
Hair held back in a clasp

The eyes level
The chin tilted off to one side

One leg extended
Fingers spread wide

An amalgam of gestures
Energy makes a round trip

BETTER YET

Business timing
Vest pocket
Display character
Rock hard
Samples of nothing
Coiled to strike
Cherry almost
Since you mention
Zen sensation
Sincerely yours

Half a column
Seen at night
Be off with you
Hold a candle to
So on's so on
End of whip
Pleased to meet
Forget about
Bring up
Stand corrected

Not a cloud
A big one
Doused in sound
From playground
Jetliner
Wind in the trees
Distant traffic
Hearing loss
Time travel
Keep in mind

As when
You come back
Glad to be
This April foolishness
Resists definition
As shade
Moves with breeze
A flicker effect
In the back
Of the mind

When in the course
Stumble onto
Under the sun
A full blast
Of extras
Cleaving to
The coast
Electronic massage
Buckminster Folsom
More where came from

Is you is
Wrong way round
Patterned after
An after party
Repeat after me
A head of steam
Brake at crossing
Ding dong school
A barking dog
Men like that

BASELINE

A week ago
I was unwinding
By poolside   .
When I lost the thread
Instead of slippage
We advocate crashage
Colliding things together
Until they break
So we can see
What they're made of

A basketball
Is made of rubber
From Peru
The upper reaches
Of the Amazon
We turn the corner
Crash into history
For discovery read slavery
Not in any book
How the West was what

It's a story made of tears
Land filling up with water
Water full of plastic
Highrise development
Along transit routes
We think about
In idle moments
The sound on concrete
Of dribbles and shots
A rickety backboard

Cars buildings toys
None of it real
People are real
Their inner workings
So difficult to apprehend
Each on an arc
From city to city
The consolidation of capital
Speaking in tongues
The Intercontinental

Every now and then
The spirit moves me
Off to one side
Everything goes on
Without me
I can write about it
When I get back
But for now
I'm just going to let
Well enough alone

DANCING COYOTE

Gray sky, low tide, wood fire
Where's your cup
Different versions of "Ask Me Now"
And "Reflections"
How about this one in 6/8
Then call England about rooms
Nothing stays the same

Let's just stay here
I'll take a shower
I don't see why not
Then we can play some music
More cool people leaving San Francisco
Bars full of white guys on phones
Light breeze in the pines

Hearing water through the wall
Cars from the road above
Locates the listener
In the here and now
Just before sailing
Off into a million thoughts
Walking away from the house

Toward music
Alive on the edge
When the speaker dies
Pack up
The rest of the day
Lies before us
Passing N. Dream Farm Road

SILHOUETTE

Seize the monument
To write down a few losses
In the state of torn paper
The declarative sentence
Is history
Outburst the order of the day
True to bent form

Tape the president back together
For posterity
If there is one
Shooting stars
Over Alabama
Have a better chance of making land
This land
Bought and sold
Many times over
In case you hadn't noticed

Table saw starts up
In adjoining yard
The poem is porous
Lets in light, sound
Anyone could write this
But would they?
Timing is something

You are halfway there
Half ear
A listening device with feet
Awake and walking
The sunny side
Delicate patterns of leaves in silhouette
The shadow of your life

That complexity
Projected on a wall
At the foot of a set of stairs

What do you know?
We'll find out later
Seize the ministry of enabled beings
The summit is brief
Barely above sea level
Shorebirds go vertical
Get the fish

Sleep stretches forward and back
An imaginary realm
Recharges your batteries
When you least expect it
The news is about as subtle
As a jackhammer at a meditation retreat
Did you say something?
The grass is yay high
You are more than welcome
And the elephant you rode in on

LEEWAY

It's Tuesday
A good day
To wait for folks
To get back to you
Meanwhile write this
My poems do or do not
Contain wildebeests

The sounds of home improvement
Shatter mere composure
What else is new

Composition is iterative
The long way round
Dreams wrap our days
In nonsensical assurance
Delirious content
Less is most
Teeming with variable feet

The sun's out
It's warmer now
The sky is sky blue

Still Tuesday
Has its ups and downs
Not to mention
The planar surface
We inhabit
As we speak
To the plants in the garden

Jet plane overhead
We do things
For multiple reasons

CONDENSATION

> "You can hope for lucky encounters only if you
> walk around a lot."—*A. J. Liebling*

You have to start from somewhere
In the interim
Is where we take place
An emptying out
Of what have you
In favor of who knows what
Very little to go on
A continuation
Without substance
A flash in the proverbial pan

Too many cooks
Watch games on TV
For there to be much feasting

The sake is extra dry
Life gets organized
At breakfast
Later falls apart completely
A blur of cities

Your war stories
Are fascinating
The raw recruits
Of my better selves
Who fan out
Over the desert
Under a penetrating sky

Death lurks underfoot
But you don't have to name it
It just is

Sometimes you let yourself coast
It doesn't take long
A light on in the kitchen
A place for everything
Not made or paid for
But dreamed up
On the spur of the moment
Then lived in
For years
Too many to remember

A BRONZE CALIPER

Texas and the Army
The subtle sensation of falling asleep
In a potato patch
Where *in* means *next*
As in next in line
Get your ticket at the station
Drink the chocolate
Pay what you owe
The great arcs of swells
Approaching the mouth of the channel

Outlines are key
According to Blake
And tie off each stanza

Each wave is only an instance
All together massive as stone
No one listens
Shorebirds make the most of it
Water under ice on Mars
Liquid water under ice sheets
And when you breathe
You are singing along
Through the centuries
Which continue to pile up outside your door

An *and* is a door to the future
T is for Tennessee
The door is ajar
Academic potatoes are cultivated in rows
Outside the bodega
A castle comprised of many smallish bottles of Miller
No one remembers this

Any two points make a line
A third, a plane
A piece of paper slid under the door
In another dimension
Talk goes on all night
Until that great author the sun
Peeks over the rim of *terra firma*

LONDON CALLING

The order of events
Or the sequence of memory
Either way
Across Westminster Bridge
The driver has praise for Las Vegas
Tired of history
Give me something totally artificial

Stuck on London Bridge
The driver lets us out in traffic
We have to hustle
To avoid oncoming bike and bus
Walk thru the City at rush hour
To the cool of St. Paul's
Their choir there

Tube from Blackfriar's
To South Kensington
Chill in hotel room
To music from the Gambia
Sona Jobarteh
A housing crisis in every city
The driver doesn't care for Goldman Sachs

White row houses on Queen's Gate
Columns columns columns
The neoclassical spans 100 years
Georges I thru IV
Plus 20th century revival
Endless accretions of form
Kaleidoscopic repetition of the gone ideal

THE AMPERSAND HOTEL

Happening across from
Mid-afternoon already
Bodies in succession
Transit routes all laid out
Easy does it
A cheap paperback
Black tank top denim cut-offs
Cool jazz in the library
Global sequencing
Temperature control

Two tables eight chairs
Present company extracted
Child sobbing in other room
Words locate the subject
The person is transparented
A voice in the middle distance
Wonder what time it is
It's right now, man
Now move on
And other unobtrusive imponderables

A glass enclosure
A straight line
A clear signal
An absolute limit
A steely resolve
An exact science
An empty cup
The moment of truth
The open door
The night to come

GRIFTER WEBINAR

Colony of global banking
Is London as per I. Sinclair
USA & UK arms
Of commercial real estate
The sun still shines
Or will
In my backyard
As the song goes
So goes the nation
A nation of clods

Happy to be here
Lapping up shade
In the interim
A holding pattern during which
Gardens grow
Up thru haze
Of wood smoke
Fog & exhaust
Toes twitch
Groceries all the way down

AUTOTUNE

One separate Monday the garden gate slammed shut
Just then the printer started up
It was a bill for surfaces rendered
Ripped crosswise or crushed in a fine mist
Every time this happens a different clergyman comes
   to call
Books pile up while doing the dishes
This side of the century needs wax
I have to *have* a hand to hand it to you
Curious about the fens
When you get home, you want to give yourself
   a good talking to

You can almost hear different things happening
Some of the smoke stained my shirt
Some do chores for a mere pittance
Some feel fear in the pit of the stomach
The whole shebang could come crashing down
There's a word for that
It's called chalcedony

Welcome to the tea room of the blank page
We've been expecting you
You'll find a bathrobe and slippers on the self

The sky opened its one door of solid oak
From the ponds the frogs called the next tune
A long one called *The Odyssey*
Parked our car right behind an ice cream truck
In honor of the joke no one got
But could never forget
We came by way of a four-lane highway
It didn't hurt much
Just about a half hour of listening

That's what's known as folk blues
You'll be pleasantly apprised
That SOS has a familiar ring
Wings of the place now scattered
Hilltops frosted with hammerings on
Every other sometime disengages the trailing carload
We live here, yes, all of us
While you're upside down get me a rhododendron

I hear a harmonica when I hardly hear at all
The wind shifts
Five o'clock shadows at noon

MAKER'S MARK

I go from one thing to another
A song, a book, a view
I can't stay long on any one thing
My energy is limited
An article on a city in Spain
The mayor has changed the center to pedestrian only
Later I'll take a walk
Hooked on sensation
Guitar strings on headphones
The complete book of Monk
Working out certain ideas
Penmanship more than capable
No stopping
Two bright lit lemons two yards away
You don't forget to breathe, do you?
The sun is continuous
The air
Bits of blue sky through the foliage
Stay with it
Not to wander wide of the mark
String beads
One color after another
Makes perfect sense
A flat plane
You can walk around on
Sun, moon, stars & sky
Everything in fours
Things build up
Fall by the wayside
Think your way out
Of introspection the very fruit
Putting one foot in front of the other
After a sandwich
Before long

Looks familiar
Sounds like something I would say
Maker's mark
Continue on down road
Pick up steam
Come back and look at this later
The sign for woman means busy person
Relax and float downstream
The guitar is building a house
A place to live in
Ink runs in and out of sync
What's said remains a mystery
Turn the corner
Turn the page
Turns out I've been listening
Seems better that way

WORD UP

Rent board
Two nouns
Over the shoulder
Then forward
Into the unknown
Socrates say
You looking for
What you already know
But don't know you know
Does this make sense
Verb phrase
Back in school
Out the window
The old rules
Throw out
Throw dice
Do not abolish chance
Do not collect 200 words
Most common English
Until the bell
Time to take
More pills
More time
Time to take more time
In doing things
While lights go on & off
As the world turns
On a turntable
More vinyl
Than China
Dig tunnel to
Does that make sense
Word perfect
Industry memory

Print on demand
The Intercontinental Railroad
Map of indigenous languages
Covers the planet
That & H2O (& CO2)
Under cover of vapor
Prepositions tell all
Relational data meet organic life
At the crossroads
Enter Elegua
Keeper of the roads
Open our eyes & see

ROOF BOOKS
the best in language since 1976

Recent & Selected Titles

- THE RESIGNATION by Lonely Christopher, 104 p. $16.95
- POLITICAL SUBJECT by Caleb Beckwith. 112 p. $17.95
- ECHOLOCATION by Evelyn Reilly, 144 p. $17.95
- HOW TO FLIT by Mark Johnson. 104 p. $16.95
- ((((...))) by Maxwell Owen Clark. 136 p. $16.95
- THE RECIPROCAL TRANSLATION PROJECT
 by Sun Dong & James Sherry. 208 p $22.95
- DETROIT DETROIT by Anna Vitale. 108 p. $16.95
- GOODNIGHT, MARIE, MAY GODHAVE MERCY ON YOUR SOUL
 by Marie Buck. 108 p. $16.95
- BOOK ABT FANTASY by Chris Sylvester. 104 p. $16.95
- NOISE IN THE FACE OF by David Buuck. 104 p. $16.95
- PARSIVAL by Steve McCaffery. 88 p. $15.95
- DEAD LETTER by Jocelyn Saidenberg. 94 p. $15.95
- social patience by David Brazil. 136 p. $15.95
- THE PHOTOGRAPHER by Ariel Goldberg. 84 p. $15.95
- TOP 40 by Brandon Brown. 138 p. $15.95
- THE MEDEAD by Fiona Templeton. 314 p. $19.95
- LYRIC SEXOLOGY VOL. 1 by Trish Salah. 138 p. $15.95
- INSTANT CLASSIC by erica kaufman 90 p. $14.95
- A MAMMAL OF STYLE by Kit Robinson
 & Ted Greenwald. 96 p. $14.95
- MOTES by Craig Dworkin. 88 p. $14.95

Roof Books are published by
Segue Foundation
300 Bowery • New York, NY 10012
For a complete list, please visit **roofbooks.com**

Roof Books are distributed by
SMALL PRESS DISTRIBUTION
1341 Seventh Street • Berkeley, CA. 94710-1403.
spdbooks.org